# Arduino Programming

A Complete Guide to Master Tools and Techniques On

Getting Started With Arduino

By

Robert Campbell

# Contents

# Introduction

An Arduino is a microcontroller development board that is open-source. In layman's terms, the Arduino may be used to control and read sensors, motors and lights. It enables you to upload programs to the board, which can subsequently interact with real-world objects. You may use this to create gadgets that respond to and respond to the outside environment. For example, if a humidity sensor linked to a plant pot becomes too dry, you may activate an automated watering system. You may also create a standalone chat server that is connected to your internet network. You can also set it to tweet whenever your cat enters or exits a pet door. You may also set your alarm to prepare a cup of coffee whenever you wake up. If anything is controlled by electricity in any way, the Arduino can interact with it somehow. Even if it isn't run on electricity, you can usually utilize items that are (such as motors and electromagnets) to interact with it. The Arduino's capabilities are almost unlimited.

Important essential features and applications of Arduino will be covered in this book.

- Description of the Arduino Board

- Installation of an Arduino

- Structure of the Arduino Program

- Data Types for Arduino

- Arduino Constants & Variables

- Arduino Programmers

- Arduino Statements of Control

- Loops for Arduino

- Arduino's Features

- Strings for Arduino

- String Object for Arduino

- Arrays on Arduino

- And there are many more.

# Chapter-1 Overview of Arduino?

Arduino is a free source programming circuit board used in several basic and complicated maker space projects. This board has a microcontroller that may be designed to detect and control items in the real world. The Arduino may interact with various outputs, including LEDs and displays, by responding to sensors and inputs. Due to its flexibility and low cost, Arduino has become a popular choice for makers and maker spaces looking to create interactive hardware projects. Massimo Bansi launched Arduino in 2005 in Italy as a method for non-engineers to use a low-cost, easy-to-use tool for making hardware projects. Because the panel is accessible for free, it is distributed by an Open-Source license, allowing anybody to make their own. Many Arduino board clones and modifications accessible on the internet; however, only authorized boards contain Arduino in their name. You'll go through a couple of Arduino boards present and how they vary in the following section.

## 1.1 Integrated Development Environment

Arduino is an open-source prototyping platform with simple hardware and software. It comprises a programable circuit board (also known as a microcontroller) and ready-to-use software known as the Arduino IDE (Integrated Development Environment), which is used to create and upload computer code to the physical board.

- Arduino boards can take analog or digital data input from various sensors and convert them to an output, such as starting a motor, turning on/off LEDs, connecting to the cloud, and various other functions.

- You may use the Arduino IDE to control the functionalities of your board by sending a list of instructions to a board's microcontroller (uploading software is referred).

- Unlike most prior customizable integrated circuits, Arduino does not require the use of a separate piece of hardware (known as a programmer) to load fresh code into the board.

- Moreover, the Arduino IDE employs a simpler model of C++, making it simpler to learn how to program. • Finally, Arduino offers a standard modular design that divides the microcontroller's functionality into a much more accessible packaging.

## 1.2 Applications of Arduino

For embedded system applications, Arduino is a breeze to utilize. Because of the Arduino open-source software, folks who do not have excellent programming abilities but want to collaborate on embedded system projects may simply utilize Arduino to build their embedded system-based projects. To start with Arduino, you need a basic understanding of electronics, such as utilizing resistors, capacitors, transistors, diodes, and other fundamental electrical components. But don't worry if you don't know anything about electronics. In the upcoming chapter of this book, you will discover all there is to know about Arduino. The following are a few Arduino applications:

- Robotics

- GSM based projects

- Ethernet-based projects

- WIFI

- Bluetooth

- And a variety of additional topics.

## 1.3 Types of Arduino Boards

Arduino is a fantastic platform for developing ideas and innovations, but choosing the proper board may be difficult. If you're new to Arduino, you may have assumed that there's just one "Arduino" board, and that was it. In truth, there are several versions of the genuine Arduino boards and hundreds of clones from rivals. But don't worry; later in this chapter, you will learn which one to start with. The following are some examples of the many kinds of Arduino boards available. The authentic Arduino boards are those with the Arduino logo on them, although there are many excellent clones on the marketplace. One of the main reasons to purchase a clone is that they are usually less costly than the original. For example, Spark Fun and Adafruit provide Arduino boards less expensive but have the same quality as the originals. One word of caution, be cautious when purchasing boards from unknown vendors.

Another thing to think about when picking a board is indeed the sort of project you want to accomplish. If you want to make a wearable electrical project, the Lilypad boards from Spark fun are a good option. The Lilypad is intended to be sewed into wearable and e-textiles crafts with ease. If your work has a compact form factor, the Arduino Pro Mini, which has a very tiny footprint comparing to other boards, can be a good choice. For analysis and analysis of the top boards available, see Spark fun's Arduino Comparison Guide. Following that, we'll look at our preferred Arduino board, which is suggested novices begin with.

**Arduino Uno**

The Arduino Uno is among the most famous Arduino boards. Even though it was not the first board to be launched, it is still the most popular and well-documented on the market. Because of its widespread usage, the Arduino Uno has many projects and forums available on the internet to assist you in getting started or getting out of a bind. Because of its amazing features and simplicity of use, You love the Uno.

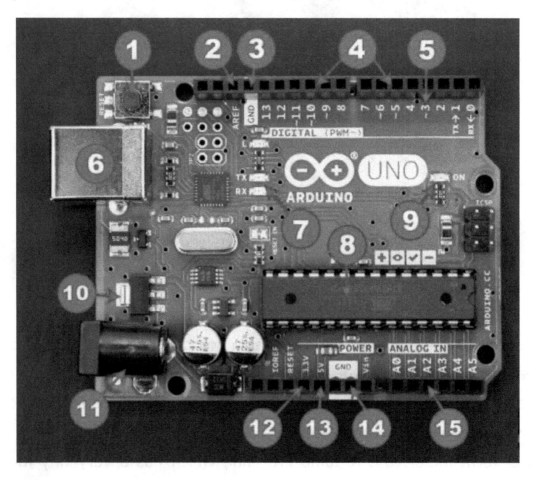

## Breakdown of the Board

The components that comprise an Arduino UNO board are listed below, along with their functionalities.

- **Reset Button.** Pressing this button will reload any programming on the Arduino board.

- **AREF**. This acronym stands for "Analog Reference," which establishes an outside reference voltage.

- **Ground Pin**. The Arduino has many ground pins, all of which function in the same way.

- **PWM.** The pins indicated with the () symbol may emulate analog output.

- **USB Cable.** Used to power up the Arduino and upload programs.

- **TX/RX.** LEDs that indicate data transmission and reception.

- **AT Mega Microchip.** It is the brain of the board, which is where the programs are kept.

- **Power Indicator Light**. When the board is hooked into a power source, this LED illuminates.

- **Voltage Regulator.** It regulates the voltage supplied to an Arduino board.

- **3.3 volts Pin.** The Pin offers 3.3 hours of electricity to your work.

- **Dc Voltage Barrel Jack.** This Pin is used to power the Arduino with such a power source.

- **V Pin**. This Pin provides your projects with 5 volts of electricity.

- **Ground Pins.** The Arduino has several ground pins that all function the same way.

- **Analog Pins**. The pins can read analog sensor signals and transform them too digital.

## Arduino Power Supply

The Arduino Uno requires a power supply to function and may be charged in several ways. You may connect the boards directly to your desktop using a USB connection, as most users do. Consider utilizing a 9V rechargeable battery to power your project if you want it to be portable. The last option is to utilize a 9V AC source of power.

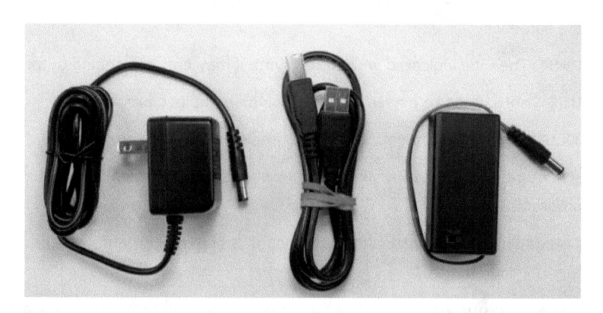

**Arduino Breadboard**

When working with Arduino, a solderless breadboard is also essential. You may use this gadget to develop your Arduino work without having to connect the circuit permanently. You may make additional prototypes and test with alternative circuit designs using a breadboard. Metal clips are joined via a strip of conductive material within the plastic housing slots (tie points).

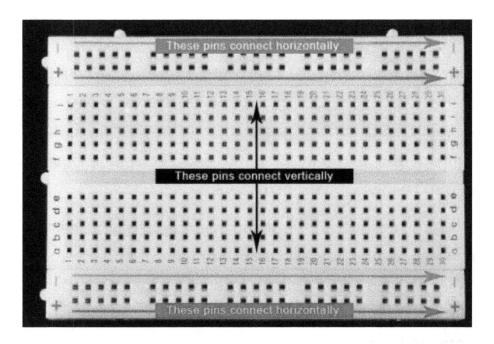

On a separate note, the breadboard does not have its power supply and must be connected to the Arduino board via jumper wires. These fibers are also used to link resistors, switches, and other elements to make the circuit.

## 1.4 How to Program Arduino

You'll have to upload the software (also called a sketch) to an Arduino after the circuit has also been built on the breadboard. The sketch is a collection of instructions that instructs the board on what tasks it must do. At any one moment, an Arduino board could only hold and execute one program. The IDE, which means for Integrated Development Environment, is the software used to build Arduino sketches. There are two essential aspects to any Arduino sketch:

**void setup ().** Sets up items that only need to be performed once and then aren't repeated.

**Void loop ().** This section contains instructions that will be repeated until the circuit is shut off.

## 1.5 Arduino – Installation

You are ready to know how to start the Arduino IDE and other major components of an Arduino UNO board. You'll be able to upload our software to the Arduino board after You've mastered this. In this chapter, you'll try to install an Arduino IDE on your computer and set up the board to get the program via USB connection in simple steps.

1st step, to begin, you'll need an Arduino board (you may use any board) and a USB wire. You'll need a conventional USB connection (A plug to B plug) if you're using an Arduino UNO, Arduino, Arduino Mega 2560, Duemilanove, or Diecimila. If you're using an Arduino Nano, you'll need to have an A to B cable instead, as seen in the picture below.

**Download Arduino IDE Software.**

From the Arduino Official Website's Download page, you may download several versions of the Arduino IDE. You must choose software that is appropriate for the OS (IOS, Windows or Linux). Unzip the file after it has finished downloading.

**Power up your board.**

The Duemilanove, Arduino Uno, Mega, and Nano automatically take power from the computer's USB port or an additional power source. If you're using the Arduino Diecimila, make sure it's set up to take power from the USB port. A jumper, a little bit of plastic that slips into two out of the three ports between the power and USB connections, is used to choose the power source. Make sure it's connected to the two pins nearest to the USB cable. Using the USB cable, attach the board to the computer. The PWR (power) LED (green) should light up.

**Launch Arduino IDE.**

You must unzip the folder after downloading the Arduino IDE program. The program icon with an infinite label may be found within the folder (application.exe). To launch the IDE, double-click the icon.

**Open your first project.**

You have two choices after the software has started:

- Begin working on a new project.

- Select a pre-existing project as an example.

- Select file>> New to start a new project.

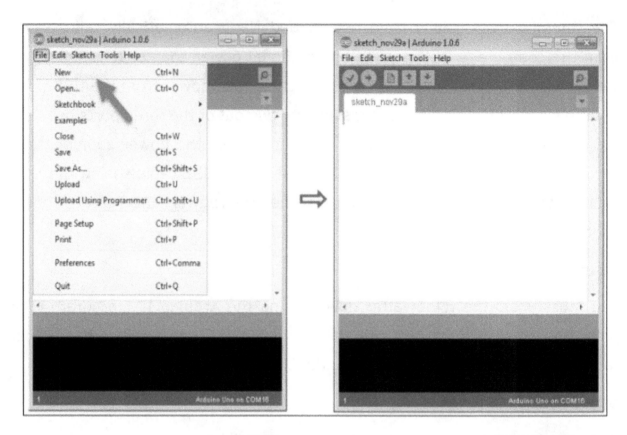

Select File >> Example >> Basics >> Blink to open an existing work example. You've chosen only one of the Blink instances for this example. It uses a timer to switch the LED off and on. Some other examples from the list may be chosen.

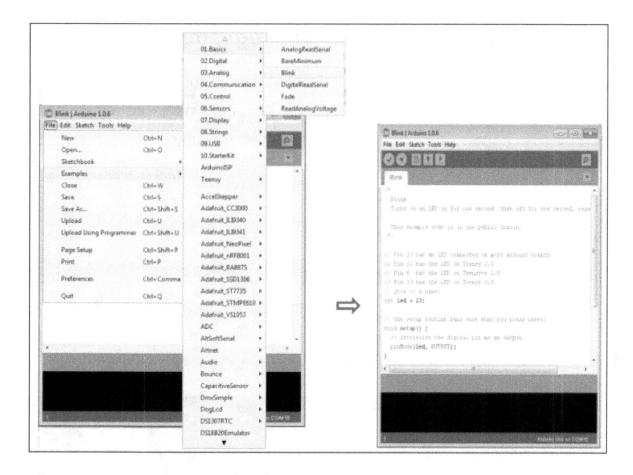

**Select your Arduino board.**

You must pick the right Arduino board name that matches the board linked to your computer to prevent errors when uploading your software to the board. Select your board from Tools >> Board.

# Chapter-2 Basic Concepts of programming

You have learned how to install your Arduino IDE, configure the appropriate USB drivers, and set up the IDE for all the Arduino Uno to be recognized in the previous chapter. We'll continue working with Arduino IDE in this chapter by examining its capabilities, learning how to use it, and uploading your first program to an Arduino UNO board.

## 2.1 Arduino IDE

Connect the Arduino Board to a computer via USB connection as indicated in the picture below and pick the proper board & COM port if not previously done before continuing with the chapter. The Arduino board does not need any external power since it pulls all of its power from the USB connection.

Sketches are the programs that run in the Arduino environment. The white region indicated in the figure below is the Text Editor in the Arduino IDE. It is where You'll write all of the code on our Arduino boards. Before you get too excited and start developing your program, you'll have a look at an example sketch included in Arduino IDE. To do so, go to the "File" menu and choose the "Examples" option. You can see a list of appropriately classified examples in the dropdown of the Examples tab, such as Basic, Analog, Digital, Communication, and so on.

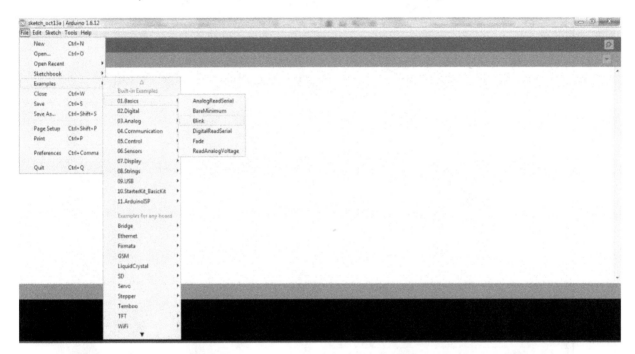

Use the simple example as a beginning or first-time user, and then pick the "Blink" sketch. The Blink drawing will be shown in a new window. You will use the Blink sketch to turn on the LED attached to the Arduino's 13th Pin for one second and then switch it off for a second in a repeating manner, i.e., you will blink the LED continually.

When You first start learning about electronics and microcontrollers, the first project or program you do is flash an LED, since flashing an LED in electronics is akin to typing Hello World in C. You will post the drawing without delving more into the programming portion of the project at this time. you need to utilize two icons in the Arduino IDE to upload the program to the Arduino board: the first is "Verify or Compile," and the second is "Upload." In the figure below, certain symbols are highlighted.

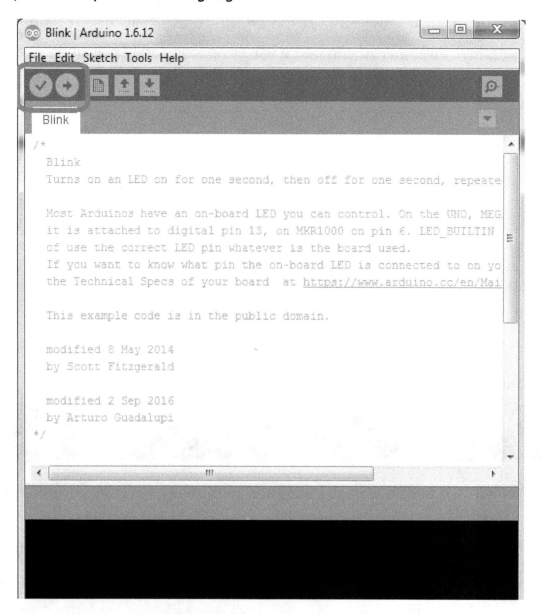

The Check or Compile symbol is the first symbol with a checkmark. You may use this icon to see whether the provided sketch is valid in terms of syntax and to see if there would be any compilation issues. You only post the drawing if the compiling is complete and error-free. To check or build the drawing, you may utilize the keyboard Ctrl + R.

The Message window is placed at the base of the IDE. It shows the compilation status, error warnings, and the specifics of the faults. You can see the progress of the compilation and the Done compiling message, and in the message window, you compile the sketch using the first icon.

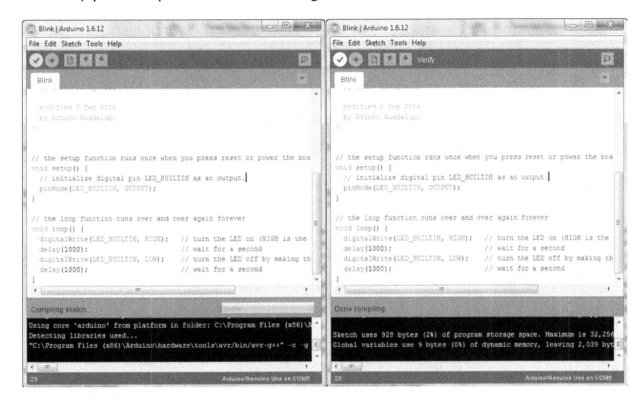

The compilation pauses at that moment if there is an issue in the sketch, such as a missing an unclosed bracket or semicolon, and the message pane displays the error with its kind and position. You may rectify the mistake using this method.

The Upload symbol is the second symbol next to the Verify symbol. Once the drawing has been successfully compiled, you may use this icon to submit it. The compiled drawing may be uploaded using the shortcut Ctrl + U. The drawing is constructed before uploading whenever You click the Upload button.

You may proceed with submitting our drawing now that it has been successfully compiled with no issues. When You click the upload tab, the sketch begins to upload, and the Arduino board's microcontroller is programmed.

The RX LEDs and TX on the Arduino UNO board will flicker during this period to indicate that data is being transferred over the serial connection. Notice in the message box that Done Uploading after the drawing has been successfully uploaded.

Other information shown in the message box includes the quantity of flash memory used by the code, the time it took to upload, and so on.

As soon as the program is successfully uploaded, the LED on the Arduino Board's 13th Pin will begin flashing with a one-second gap (According to the sketch written).

You learned how to upload your first sketch to the Arduino Board and about some of the Arduino IDE's fundamental capabilities.

## 2.2 Arduino Program Analysis

You saw how to configure the Arduino IDE, build (or validate) the code, upload the program to an Arduino UNO board, and verify for error messages in the earlier section of the book. All of this was shown with the aid of the Arduino IDE's sample program "Blink."

You'll attempt to comprehend the Blink program, its components, its syntax, and some preset functions in this chapter. You will also experiment with modifying the basic Blink sketch to see how they affect the output.

To do so, launch the blink program in the Arduino IDE (and with Arduino Board currently attached to the computer). You can notice some grey lines at the top of the drawing and some colorful lines at the draw base. Each Arduino sketch (or, for that matter, any program, regardless of programming language) is made up of a series of reference lines called comments and the actual code.

## 2.3 Arduino Code for Beginners

C++ is the Arduino programming language. The majority of the time, users will utilize a limited subset of C++ that resembles C. If you're acquainted with Java, you'll find C++ to be simple to use and understand. Do not be concerned or worried if you've never coded before. You'll find everything you have to get started in the next paragraphs. C++'s most significant "high-level" feature is that this is object-oriented. An object is a concept in such a language that mixes functional code (code that performs computations and memory operations) with "state" code (the results of such simple values or calculations stored in variables).

Compared to previous paradigms, object orientation enabled programming to be somewhat more productive in certain applications since it enabled programmers to design complex programs using abstractions.

An Ethernet adapter, for example, might be represented as an object with properties (such as its IP and MAC addresses) and capabilities (like asking a DHCP server for network configuration details). Object-oriented programming became the most popular programming paradigm, and C++ has had a significant effect on most current languages, including Java, Ruby, and Python. You'll be referring to libraries containing object definitions (called "classes") in a lot of the sketch code you'll be authoring and viewing. Your original code will be made up of "glue" code and modifications to a significant degree. By studying a tiny part of C++, you can indeed be productive nearly immediately.

The code that comprises your sketch must be turned into machine code which the Arduino's microcontroller understands. A compiler is a particular software that does the compilation. You don't have to worry more about intricacies since the Arduino IDE comes with just an open-source C++ compiler. Consider this: once you click the "Upload" button, the IDE launches the compiler, which turns your human-readable instructions into ones and zeros before sending it all to the microcontroller through USB.

C++, like any other effective programming language, has a variety of terms and constructions. Constructors, operators, Conditionals, functions, data structures, variables, and many other things are available.

You will learn about the architecture of an Arduino program, functions, and variables in this chapter. Take a few moments to absorb this new information before moving on to the last session, in that you will understand how to program the Arduino to make choices and communicate with the outside environment.

## 2.4 An Arduino sketch

The simplest Arduino sketch imaginable is

```
void setup(){

printf("hello"); // setup code, run once:

}

void loop(){

printf("hello"); // main code run repeatedly:

}
```

There are two functions in this code.

- The first one has been put up (). When the program begins, everything you enter in this function would be performed either by Arduino just once.

- Loop is the second (). When the Arduino finishes executing the instructions in the setup () method, it will enter a loop () and continue executing it in a loop until you reboot it or turn off the power.

Take note of the close and open parenthesis in setup () and loop (). Functions may accept arguments, which allows the program to communicate information across its many functions. There are no arguments supplied to the loop and setup procedures. If you put anything inside the parenthesis, the compiler will report a compile error and halt the compilation process. Even if you don't utilize them, these two functions will be present in every drawing you produce.

Removing one of them will result in an error notice from the compiler. These are two of the Arduino language's minimal requirements. The two functions are essential, but you may create your own if you like. Let's have a look at the following point.

## 2.5 Custom functions

A function is nothing more than a collection of instructions with such a name. The Arduino IDE requires your sketch to have the loop () and setup () routines, but you may create your own. Organizing your drawings by grouping instructions within functions is an excellent idea, particularly as they grow more complex as you gain confidence as a programmer. A definition and the code that fits within the curly brackets are required to define a function. At least the following is included in the definition.

- one return type

- a name

- a parameter list

```
int calc(int x, int y)
{
    int z = x + y;
    return z;
}
```

In the first line, the return type is int. It instructs the compiler that the caller will get an integer value (the function Called).

The function's name (also referred to as its "identifier") is doing a calc. You may name the functions anything you want as long as you don't use a reserved term (that is, a term already in use by the Arduino language), there are no spaces, and special characters like percent, $, and # aren't used. A number cannot be used as the initial character. If in doubt, keep in mind that function names should only include numbers, letters, and the underscore.

You establish a new integer-type variable during the first line of the coding (int). The result of adding x and y is assigned to z.

Finally, you return the value saved in z to the caller of calc in the two lines of the function's body. Let's imagine you want to use your setup function to call calc. Here's a detailed example of how to accomplish it:

```
void setup()
{
  // setup code, to run only once:
    int z = calc(8,12);
```

```
}
void loop()
{
    // main code, to execute it repeatedly:
}
int calc(int x, int y)
{
    int z = x + y;
    return z;
}
```

The second line of the setup () method declares a variable, x. It calls the method calc on the same line and sends the numbers 8 and 12 to it. The calc function adds the two integers together and delivers the result 3 to a caller, the setup () method's second line. The number 20 is then saved in variable z, and the setup () method is completed.

## 2.6 Comments

Comments can be found on any line that begins with / or paragraph (contain multiply lines) that begin with /* and end with */. The compiler disregards comments. They are intended for the coder to read. Comments are being used to explain how code works or leave remarks for other developers (or self).

There is indeed a definition of a parameter with the identifier in the setup () method. There is also a definition of a variable with the same identifier in function calc (The fact that this definition is on the function definition block makes no difference).). It's not an issue to have variables to the same name as long as they're not even in the same target. The curly brackets determine the scope. Within that scope would be any variable between being an open and closed curly bracket. There is no contradiction if there is indeed a variable with the same name declared in another scope.

When choosing a name for the variables, be cautious. Scope issues may be a pain: you can think a variable is available at a certain point in your sketch just to discover it is out of range. Also, make sure your variables have appropriate descriptive names. If you wish to save the value of a pin in a variable, name it something like:

```
int p = 0; // p should be replacing with pin,
```

## 2.7 Data Types

In C, data types refer to a comprehensive system for defining variables and functions of various kinds. The category of a variable dictates how much storage space it takes up and how the stored bit pattern is interpreted. The table below lists all of the data categories that you'll encounter when programming with Arduino.

**void**

Only function declarations utilize the void keyword. It denotes that the function should return no data to the function of which it was invoked.

Example

```
Void Loop (){
   // Set of code should be written here.

}
```

**Boolean**

True (1) or false (0) are the only two possible values for a Boolean. One byte of storage memory is used for each Boolean variable.

Example

`boolean val = false;` // declaration, initial value of variable be false

`boolean state = true;` // declaration, initial value of state be True

## Char

A character value is stored in the data type, which takes up a single byte of memory. Single quotes are used for character literals, such as 'A,' while double quotes are used for strings with several characters, such as "ABC."

Characters, on the other hand, are kept as integers. In the ASCII chart, you can observe the particular encoding. It implies that mathematical operations on characters may be performed using the ASC-II value of the character. Because the ASC-II forms of capital character A are 65, 'A' + 1 also has 66.

## Example

`Char xhar1 = 'a'` ;// declaration, initial value of variable(char) be a

`Char xhar1= 97` ;// declaration, initial value of variable(char) be 97

## unsigned char

It is also an unsigned type of data with a one-byte memory footprint. Numbers ranging from 0 to 255 are encoded using unsigned char data type.

Example

Unsigned Char Xchar1 = 225; // declaration, initial value of variable(char) be a 225

## byte

A byte stores an 8-bit unsigned number, from 0 to 255.

Example

```
byte m = 25;//declaration of a variable with type byte and initialize it.
```

## int

Integers are the most used data type for storing numbers. A 16-bits (2-byte) result is calculated in int. It results in -32,768 - 32,767 (with a minimum of -$2^{15}$ and a maximum of ($2^{15}$) - 1).

The int size changes depending on the board. An int, for example, on the Arduino Due saves a 4-byte (32-bit) value. The result ranges from -2147483648 - 2,147,483,647 (with a minimum of -$2^{31}$ and a maximum of ($2^{31}$) - 1).

```
int num1 = 232 ;// declaration, initial value of variable(int) be 232
```

## Unsigned int

Unsigned ints hold a two-byte value in the same manner as ints do. They don't store negative integers, instead just positive ones, giving them a usable range of 0- 65,535 ($2^{16}$) - 1. The Due saves a four-byte (32-bit) value that may range from 0-4,294,967,295 ($2^{32}$ - 1) value.

```
Unsigned int numbr1 = 560;// declaration, initial value of variable(int) be 560
```

## Word

A word holds a 16-bits unsigned number on the Arduino and other ATMEGA-based devices. It saves a 32-bits unsigned integer on the Due or Zero.

Example

```
word x = 5160 ;// declaration, initial value of variable(word) be 5160
```

## Long

Long variables hold 32 bits (4 bytes) and range-2,147,483,648-2,147,483,647, are enhanced size variables for number storage.

Example

`Long speed = 589696`; / declaration, initial value of variable(long) be 589696

**short**

A 16-bit data type is referred to as a short. A brief saves a 16-bit (2-byte) value on all Arduinos (ARM and AT-Mega based). It results in a range of -32,768 - 32,767 (with a minimum of $-2^{15}$ and a maximum of $(2^{15})$ - 1).

Example

`short num = 114;` / declaration, initial value of variable(long) be 114

**float**

A number with a decimal point is the data type for a floating-point number. Because it offers more resolution than integers, floating-point integers are often employed to approximate analog and continuous quantities.

Floating-point numbers may range in size from 3.4028235E+38 - -3.4028235E+38. They are represented as 32 bits of data (4 bytes).

Example

`float pi = 3.14;` /declaration of a float variable with 3.14 as its initial value

**double**

Double-precision floating-point numbers take up four bytes on the Uno and other ATMEGA-based boards. That is, a double implementation is identical to the float implementation, with no increased inaccuracy. Doubles mostly on Arduino Due have an 8-bytes which is equal to (64-bit) precision.

Example.

double num = 256.342;/ declare a double variable and initialize it with 256.342

## 2.8 Variables

When it comes to data processing, a program is really handy. Data processing is something that programs perform all of the time. Either a user will provide data for the program to process or generate its data (possibly via a keypad). From a sensor (such as a temperature thermistor), the network (such as a cloud computer), a local shared folder (such as a Memory Card), a local memory (such as an EPROM), and a variety of additional locations.

Regardless of where your software obtains its data, it must keep it in memory to function with it. Variables are used to do this. A variable is indeed equipment that assigns a name to a memory region (an identifier). You utilize an easy-to-remember moniker instead of the memory location's address in our software. You've previously encountered a variable. You have created several variables, x, y, and z, containing an integer in the previous section on custom functions.

Other than numbers, variables may contain a variety of data. A couple of these are built-in to the Arduino language (that, recall, is C++).

A valid name and type are required to create a variable. A valid name has an underscore, letters, and numbers that begin with a character and is not reserved, much like functions. Here's an illustration:

```
byte sensor_B_value;
```

This line creates the sensor_B_value variable, which will store a single byte into memory. You may store data in it in the following way:

```
sensor_B_value = 1596;
```

This value may be printed to a serial monitor as follows:

```
serial.print(sensor_B_value);
```

The serial display is an Arduino IDE feature that enables you to show text from the Arduino on your screen. You will go into more detail about this later, but for now, you want to demonstrate how to access the hash value in a variable. Simply say its name. Remember what you said about scope earlier: the variable must be inside scope once it is invoked.

A variable's value may also be changed, which is one of its most appealing features. You may update the variable by taking a fresh reading from the sensor as follows:

```
sensor_B_value = 221;
```

There's no issue; the old value has vanished, and the new value has been saved.

## 2.9 Constants

If there is a value in your drawing that will not change, label it as a constant. Constants provide memory and processing performance advantages, and it is a good practice to employ them. You may use the following syntax to declare a constant:

```
const int sen_pin = 0;
```

You give the variable sen_pin a name, indicate that as constant, and setting it to 0. You'll receive a compiler error warning if you attempt to alter the value later.

## Operators

O Operators are functions that act on a single or several bits of data.

The fundamental arithmetic operations, = (assign), +, -, *, and /, are recognisable to most individuals. There are, however, many more. The following are some of the most regularly used operators: The software will not be uploaded to an Arduino at all.

**"%" Modulo**

It is a mathematical operator in which remainder is returned after division

Consider the following scenario: 5% 2 = 1

**+=, -=, *=, /= Compound operator.**

It executes the code on a variable's current value.

Example

`int x = 15;  x+= 3;`

Consequently, a containing 18 will be produced (the original 15 plus a three from the addition operation).

**++, --**

It will increase or decrease the value of a variable by 1

Example

`int x = 15; x++;`

The answer will be 16.

**Comparison operators.  ==, !=, <, >, <=, >=**

Based on the comparison result, comparison operators will produce a Boolean (true or false).

== means equality

! = means un-equality

< means less than

> means greater than

<= means less than or equal to

>= means greater than or equal t.

Example

```
int x = 15;
```

```
int y== 6;
```

Boolean x = y == z; As a consequence, variable c will have a false (0) boolean value. The compound assignment operators will always give true (1) and false (0) results.

## NOT (!), AND (&&), OR (||)

Operators that are logical. Using the "!" operator, you may reverse a boolean value. && AND of two Booleans || OR of two Booleans ||. AND give 1 means true all all the inputs variable are 1 or true otherwise false. OR operation will give 0 or false if all the input variables is zero or false.

```
boolean x = true;
```

```
boolean y = true;
```

```
boolean z = false;
```

```
boolean a = !x; // a  will give false
```

```
boolean b = y && x; // b will give false
```

```
boolean c = y || z; // z  will give true
```

There are others as well. Bitwise operators may be used to operate at the bit level, such as manipulating individual bits inside a byte (which is helpful for stuff like shift registers). However, that's something you may learn afterward.

# Chapter-3: I/O Functions

The Arduino board's pins can be used as both inputs or outputs. We'll go through how the pins operate in various modes. It's worth noting that most Arduino analog pins can be set and utilized in the same way as digital pins can.

## 3.1 Pins as INPUT

When utilizing Arduino pins as inputs, they are already set up as inputs and do not have to be explicitly designated as inputs using pinMode(). High-impedance pins are those that have been configured in this manner. Input pins place incredibly low requirements on the circuit they're sampling, the equivalent of a 100 megaohm series resistor at the front of the Pin.

It implies that switching the input pin from one state to the other requires relatively little current. As a result, the pins may build a touch sensor or scan a LED as just a photodiode.

With nothing attached to it or wires attached to It that are not linked to other circuits, pins set as pinMode (Pin, INPUT) report random adjustments in pin state, taking up electrical distortion from the environment capacitively connecting the state of a neighboring pin.

## 3.2 Pull-up Resistors

When no input is provided, the pull-up resistor is often used to guide input signals to the predefined condition. On the input, a pull-up resistance (to +5V) or a pull-down resistor (to ground) may be used to accomplish this. For just a pull-down or pull-up resistor, a 10K ohm resistor is an excellent choice.

## 3.3 Pull-up Resistor as Input

The At-mega chip has 20,000 pull-up resistors that may be accessed by software. Set the pinMode() to INPUT PULL-UP to access the built-in pull-up resistors. It reverses the behavior of an INPUT mode, in which HIGH indicates that the sensor is turned off and LOW indicates that it is turned on. The pull-value up's is determined by the microcontroller utilized. The value of most AVR-based boards is certified to be between $20,000 and $50,000. It is between 50k and 150k on the Arduino Due. Consult the datasheet for the microcontroller of your board for the specific value.

When attaching a sensor to an INPUT PULL-UP pin, make sure the other end is connected to the ground. It enables the Pinto to indicate HIGH whenever the switch is turned off and LOW because it is pushed in a basic switch. The pull-up resistors supply enough current to illuminate an LED attached to an input pin faintly. It is most likely what is going on if LEDs inside a design seem to be operating, but only very weakly.

The pull-up resistors are controlled by the same registers (internal chip location) that control whether a bit is HIGH or LOW. As a result, if a pin is also programmed to have pull-up resistors when in input mode, the Pin will be set as HIGH when moved to an OUTPUT mode using pinMode (). If an output pin is set in a HIGH state and switched to an input using pinMode, the pull-up resistor will be set ().

```
pinMode(5,INPUT) ; // <set pin as input not with the help of built resistor>
pinMode(3,INPUT_PULLUP) ; // <set pin as input not with the help of built resistor>
```

## 3.4 Pins as OUTPUT

Low-impedance pins are those that have been set as OUTPUT using pinMode(). It implies they can deliver a significant quantity of electricity to other circuits. Atmega pins may deliver up to 40 milliamps of electricity to external devices/circuits as a source (positive current) or sink (negative current). It is sufficient current to illuminate an LED (remember the series resistor) brilliantly or power several sensors, but not enough to power relays, motors or solenoids.

Attempting to power high-current devices from output pins may harm or kill the Pin's output transistors, as well as the Atmega chip as a whole. It often leads to a "dead" bit in the microcontroller, although the other chips continue to work properly. As a result, unless maximum current taken from the pins is necessary for a specific application, it is a smart option to link the OUTPUT pins to many other devices with 470 or 1k resistors.

### pinMode() Function

The pinMode() method is used to specify whether a pin should be utilized as an output or an input. The mode INPUT PULL-UP may be used to activate the internal pull-up resistors. In addition, the internal pull-ups are expressly disabled in the INPUT mode.

Syntax.   `pinMode()`

Example

```
Void setup(){pinMode(pin,mode);
}
```

- mode OUTPUT, INPUT, or INPUT_PULLUP
- pin the number of a pin which mode you want to change

```
int button=3 ; // button linked to pin 3

int LED=4; // LED linked to pin 4

void setup() {pinMode(button , INPUT_PULLUP);// input with pull-up resistor

pinMode(button,OUTPUT); // pin as output

}

void setup(){

If(digitalRead(button) == HIGH)

{

digitalWrite(LED,LOW);

delay(300); //300 ms delay

digitalWrite(LED,HIGH);

delay(300); //300 ms delay

}

}
```

## digitalWrite() Function

To write a LOW or HIGH value to a digital pin, use the digitalWrite() method. If pinMode() has been used to establish the Pin as an OUTPUT, the voltage would be configured to the appropriate value, 5V (3.3V for 3.3V board) for HIGH, for LOW 0V (ground) If the Pin is set to INPUT, digitalWrite() will activate (HIGH) or deactivate (LOW) the input pin's internal pull-up. The internal pull-up resistance should be enabled by setting pinMode() to INPUT PULL-UP.

When executing digitalWrite(HIGH), if pinMode() is not set to OUTPUT, and an LED is connected to a pin, the LED may seem faint. DigitalWrite() will have activated the inbuilt pull-up resistor, which operates as a big current-limiting resistor if pinMode() is not explicitly set.

Syntax digitalWrite()

```
Void loop(){

digitalWrite(pin,value);

}
```

- PIN, which is the number of a pin which mode you want to change

- value, which is either HIGH or LOW

```
int LED = 3; // LED linked to pin 3

void setup( {

pin_Mode(LED,OUTPUT); // set as output

}

void setup(){

digitalWrite(LED,HIGH);

delay(300); // 300 ms delay

digitalWrite(LED,LOW);

delay(500); // 500 ms delay

}
```

**analogRead( ) function**

The digitalRead() method on the Arduino may detect if a potential is applied to its pins and display it. An off/no sensor (that senses the presence of an item) differs from an analog sensor, whose value changes constantly. A different sort of Pin is required to read this sort of sensor.

Six pins labeled "Analog In" are located in the lower-right corner of the Arduino board. These particular pins indicate whether or not potential is applied to it and the magnitude of that voltage. You may read the applied voltage to one of the pins using the analogRead() method. This method returns a value from 0 to 1023, corresponding to voltages of 0 to 5 volts. When a 2.5 V voltage is supplied to pin 0, for example, analogRead(0) returns 512.

Syntax analogRead()

```
analogRead(pin);
```

pin specifies the input pin pin to read via (0-7 on the Mini boards ,0-5 on most boards, 0-5 on the Mega)

Example

```
int analogPin=4;  //Linked to analog pin 3
int num = 0; // Store read value
void setup(){
    Serial.begin(8600); // setup
}
void loop() {
    num = analogRead(analogPin); // read the pin
    Serial.println(val); // debug
}
```

## 3.5 Arduino - Advanced I/O Function

Advanced output, as well as input functions will be covered.

**Analogous Reference()**

It is a function that returns a list of references

Configures the analog input reference voltage (the value used as the top of the input range). The possibilities are as follows:

- The default analogue reference is 5 volts (for 5V Arduino) or 3.3 v (on 3.3V Arduino) (on 3.3V Arduino)

- INTERNAL 1.1 volts upon on ATmega168 or ATmega328, and 3 volts on the ATmega8

- A built-in 1.1V reference, INTERNAL1V1 (Arduino Mega only)

- A built-in 3V reference is INTERNAL2V56 (Arduino Mega only)

- EXTERNAL The reference is the voltage provided to an AREF pin (0-5V only).

Syntax

- analogReference()

- analogReference (type);

Any kind of the following may be used (EXTERNAL, DEFAULT, INTERNAL2V56, INTERNAL, INTERNAL1V1)

The external voltage level mostly on the AREF pin should not be much less than 0V or greater than 5V. You should set the analog referencing to EXTERNAL before using the analogRead() method if you're utilizing an external level on the AREF pin. Otherwise, you risk harming your Arduino board's microprocessor by shorting the active voltage level (internally produced) and the AREF pin.

Analog reference pin

You may also use a 5K resistor to link the exterior voltage level to the AREF pin, enabling you to toggle among internally and externally reference voltages.

Because there are inbuilt 32K resistors on the AREF pin, the resistor will change the voltage used as the reference. The two works together to create a voltage divider. 2.5V passed via the resistor, for example, will result in $2.5*32/(32+5)=2.2V$ only at the AREF pin.

Example

```
int analogPin=4;
int num=0;
void setup(){
Serial.begin(9600);
analogReference(EXTERNAL
//reference.
}
```

```
void loop(){

val = analogRead(analogPin); // read the input pin

Serial.println(val); // debug value

}
```

# 3.6 Character Functions

All data is inputted into the computer as characters, including letters, numerals, or other special symbols. The abilities of C++ for analyzing and modifying individual characters are discussed in this chapter

Several methods in the character-handling library provide helpful checks or manipulations of specific types of data. As a parameter, each function gets a character, expressed as just an int, or EOF. Integers are often used to alter characters.

Remember that EOF is generally set to −1 and that certain hardware designs prohibit the storage of negative values in char variables. As a result, the character-handling routines work with characters as if they were integers.

The functionalities of the character-handling module are summarized in the table below. Include the cctype>>header while using operations from the character-handling library.

**int isdigit(int x )**

If x is a digit, it returns 1; otherwise, it returns 0.

**int isalpha(int x )**

If x is a letter, it returns 1; otherwise, it returns 0.

**int isalnum(int x )**

If x is a letter or digit, it returns 1; otherwise, it returns 0.

### int isxdigit(int x )

If x is a hexadecimal digit, it returns 1; otherwise, it returns 0.

### int islower(int x )

If x is a lowercase letter, it returns 1; otherwise, it returns 0.

### int isupper(int x )

If x is an uppercase letter, it returns 1; otherwise, it returns 0.

### int isspace(int x )

If x is a white-space character horizontal tab ('t'), (newline ('n'), form feed ('f'), carriage return ('r'), space (' '), vertical tab ('v'), it returns 1; otherwise, it returns 0.

### int iscntrl(int x)

If x is a controlled character like horizontal tab ('t'), (newline ('n'), form feed ('f'), carriage return ('r'), space (' '), vertical tab ('v'),  it returns 1; otherwise, it returns 0.

### int ispunct(int x )

If x is a printed character apart from space, a numeral, or a letter, it returns 1; otherwise, it returns 0.

### int isprint(int x)

If x is a printed character that includes a space (' '), it returns 1; otherwise, it returns 0.

### int isgraph(int x )

If x is a printing letter apart from space (' '), it returns 1; otherwise, it returns 0.

**Example**

The functions isalnum, isdigit, isalpha, and isxdigit are shown in the following example. The isdigit function checks if the parameter is just a digit (0–9). The isalpha function detects if the parameter is an uppercase (A-Z) or lowercase (a–z) character. The isalnum function checks if the parameter is an uppercase, lowercase, or digit. If the input is a hexadecimal digit (A–F, a–f, 0–9), the function isxdigit returns true.

```
void setup(){
Serial.begin(9600);// Open the port at data rate to 9600 bps
Serial.print("\rIsdigit:\r");  // commants
Serial.print(isdigit('9')?"\r9":"9 not\r");
Serial.print("\rdigit\r"); //
Serial.print(isdigit('9')?"#is-a":"#is-not-a\r") ;
Serial.print("\rdigit\r");
Serial.print("\rIsalpha:\r" );
  Serial.print(isalpha('B' ) ?"A_is _a": "A_is _ot_a");
  Serial.print("letter\r");
  Serial.print(isalpha('B' ) ?"b_is_a": "b_is_not_a");
  Serial.print("letter\r");
  Serial.print(isalpha('B') ?"&_is_a": "&_is_not-a");
  Serial.print(" letter\r");
```

```cpp
  Serial.print(isalpha('B' )?"4_is_a":"4_is_not_a");

  Serial.print("\rletter\r");

  Serial.print("\risalnum:\r");

  Serial.print(isalnum('A' ) ?"A_is_a":"A_is_not_a" );

  Serial.print("digit_or_a_letter\r");

  Serial.print(isalnum('8')?"\r8_is_a\r":"8_is_not_a");

  Serial.print("\rdigit_or_a_letter\r");

  Serial.print(isalnum('#')?" \r #is a":"#is_not_a\r ");

  Serial.print("\r digit_or_ a_ letter\r");

  Serial.print("\rIsxdigit:\r");

  Serial.print(isxdigit('F')?" \r F_is _a":"_ is_not_a" );

  Serial.print(" \r  hexadecimal_digit\r" );

  Serial.print(isxdigit('J')?"J is a":"J_is_not-a");

  Serial.print("\r  hexadecimal digit\r");

  Serial.print(isxdigit('7')?"7_is_a":"7_is_not_a");

  Serial.print(" \r  hexadecimal_digit\r");

  Serial.print(isxdigit('$' )?" \r  $_is_a":"$_is_not_a" );

  Serial.print(" \r  hexadecimal digit\r");

  Serial.print(isxdigit('f )?" \r f_is_a":"f_is_not_a");

}

void loop () {

}
```

**Result**

Isdigit:

8 digit

# not

Isalpha:

A_is_a_letter

B_is_a_letter

&_Is_not_a _etter

4_is_not_a_letter

isalnum:

A_is_a_digit_or_a_letter

8_is_a_digit_or_a_letter

#_is_not_a_digit_or_a_letter

isxdigit:

F_is_a_hexadecimal_digit

J_is_not_a_hexadecimal_digit

7_is_a_hexadecimal_digit

$_i_not_a_hexadecimal_digit

F_is_a_hexadecimal_digit

For each letter examined, You just use conditional operator (?:) to decide if the text " is a " or the phrase " is not a " should be written in the output. Line a, for example, shows that the text "8 is a " is written if '8' would be a digit—

that is when isdigit gives a true (non-zero) result. The text " 8 is not a " is written when '8' would not be a digit (i.e., when isdigit returns 0).

# Chapter-4 Control Statements, Loops, Functions and Strings

You will learn control statements that control the flower of execution, a loop that executes a set of repeated statements in this chapter,.

## 4.1 Control Statements

The programmer must define one or more criteria to be examined or checked by the program using decision-making structures. It should be accompanied by the statements that will be performed if the condition is true, and optionally, additional statements will be performed if the condition is false.

The general shape of a common decision-making framework present in most programming languages is shown below.

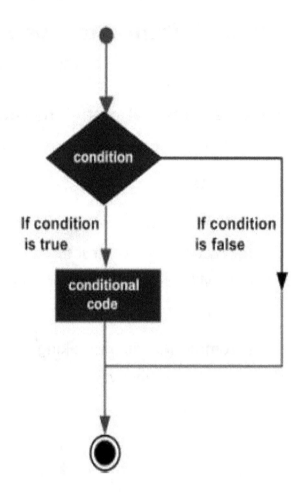

### If statement

It accepts a parenthesis-enclosed phrase as well as a statement or set of statements. The block of statements or statements is performed if another expression is true; else, the statements are skipped.

### If ...else statement

When the condition is false, an if statement might be preceded via an optional else statement.

### If...else if ...else statement

When the condition is false, an if statement might be preceded via an optional else statement.

**switch case statement**

Switch...case, like if statements, regulates the flow of the program by letting programmers declare distinct instructions that should be performed under different circumstances.

**Conditional Operator?**

What's with the conditional operator? In C, there is just one ternary operator.

## 4.2 Loops

Different control structures are available in programming languages, allowing for more sophisticated execution routes.

In most programming languages, a loop statement enables an instruction or a collection of statements several times, and below is the basic idea of a loop statement. The C programming language includes the following kinds of loops.

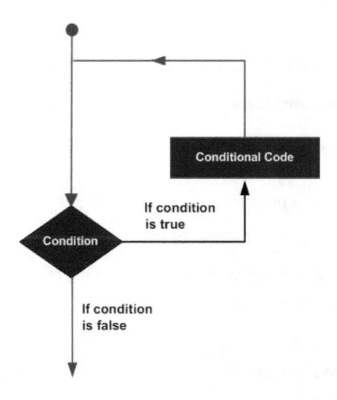

**while loop**

While loops continue to loop indefinitely until the expression within the parenthesis, (), turns false. The tested variable must be changed, and else the while loop would never end.

**do...while loop**

The while loop and the do...while loop is similar. The path is verified at the start of the while loop before the content of the iteration is executed.

**for loop**

A for loop repeats statements a certain number of times. The for-loop parentheses are used to set up, test, and change the loop's control expression.

**Nested Loop**

The C programming language enables you to nest loops. Loop inside a loop.

**Infinite loop**

It's a loop that doesn't have a way to end. Therefore it becomes endless.

## 4.3 Arduino - Functions

Functions enable you to break down the program into smaller chunks of code that accomplish specific functions. When you need to do the same action numerous times in a program, you should create a function.

Organizing source code into functions provides several benefits.

- Functions aid in the programmer's organization. It often helps in the conceptualization of the program.

- Functions codify one operation in one place, reducing the number of times a function should be thought about it and debugged, as well as the number of times the code must be modified.

- Because chunks of code were reused several times, functions make the entire sketch shorter and more compact.

- They make it simpler to buffeted in those other programs by keeping it modular, and they make it more understandable by employing functions.

The loop () and setup () procedures are both necessary inside an Arduino ide or program (). Outside of the brackets of such two functions, new functions must be constructed. The most often used syntax for defining a function is.

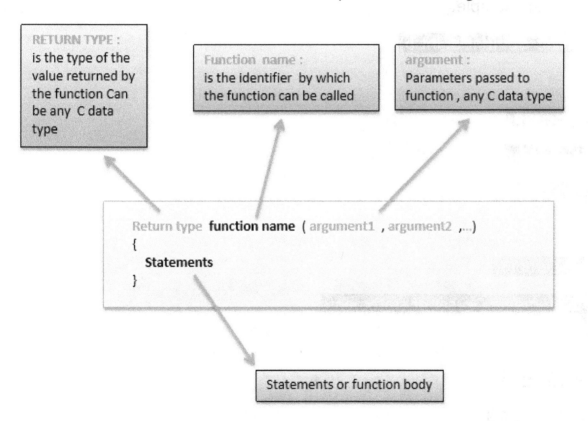

## 4.4 Function Declaration

A function is defined below or above the loop function, outside of any other functions.

You have two options for declaring the function.

The simplest method is to simply write the component of the function known as a function prototype just above loop function, that consists of the following:

• Function return type

• Function name

• Function argument type (the argument name does not need to be written)

• Function prototype must be followed by a semicolon ( ; ).

The first technique is used to demonstrate the function declaration in the following example.

```
int func_Sum(int a, int b)
{
    int c = 1;
    c = a+b ;
    return c;
}
void setup(){
    Statements Or  set of statements
}
Void loop(){
int result = 0;
result =func_sum(12,12) ;
}
```

The second section, known as the function declaration or definition, must be declared just below the loop function, and it consists of the following elements:

- Function return type

- Function name

- Function argument type (where the argument name must be included).

The body's function (statements in the function where it is calling for executing)

```
int Func_Sub(int a, int b);
void setup(){
A statement or set of statements
}
void loop(){
    int subtraction = 0;
    subtraction = Func_Sub(15,6);
}
int Func_mul(int g, int j)
int q = 0;
q = g*j;
return q; // return the value
}
```

## 4.5 Strings

Text is stored using strings. They may be used to show text on an LCD or even in the Serial Monitor window of the Arduino IDE. Strings may also be used to store user input. For instance, the characters which a user writes on an Arduino-connected keypad.

In Arduino programming, there are two sorts of strings:

- Character arrays, which are similar to strings in C programming.

- The Arduino String object, which allows us to utilize the string object in our sketches.

You will learn about strings, objects, and how to utilize them in Arduino projects in this chapter. You'll know which sort of string to utilize in a drawing.

## 4.6 String Character Arrays

The first sort of string we'll study is a string that consists of a sequence of char characters. You learned how an array is in the last chapter: a sequence of the same data stored in the memory. A string is a collection of character variables. A string is a unique array with an important addition only at the end of a string that is always set to 0. (zero). A "null-ended string" is what this is called.

**Example of String Array**

```
void setup(){
char exm_str[5];
Serial.begin(9600);
exm_str[0] = 't';
exm_str[1]= 'h';
exm_str[2] = 'e';
exm_str[3] = 'a';
exm_str[4] = 'l';
exm_str[5] = 'i';
Serial.println(exm_str);
```

```
}
```

```
void loop() {
```

```
}
```

The following example demonstrates how a string comprises a character array containing printable characters with 0 as the array's final member to indicate that the string terminates here. Using Serial. println() and giving the string's name, the string may be printed to the Arduino Serial Monitor window.

```
void setup() {
```

```
char exm_str [] = "Hello";
```

```
Serial.begin(9600);
```

```
Serial.println(exm_str);
```

```
}
```

```
void loop() {
```

```
}
```

The compiler estimates the size of a string array in this sketch and automatically null terminating the string with a zero. The same method is used to build a six-element array comprised of 5 characters preceded by zero, as in the preceding illustration.

## 4.7 Manipulating String Arrays

As seen in the following sketch, you may change a string array inside a drawing.

```
void setup () {
```

```
char love [] = "I love You";
```

```
Serial.begin(9600); // (1) printing the string

Serial.println(love); // (2) deleting the string

love[2] = 0;

Serial.println(love);   //(3) substitute string

love [13] = ' ';

love[18] = 'b'; // insert the new word

love[19] = "o";

love[20] = 'o';

love[21] = k;

Serial.println(love);

}

void loop() {

}
```

**Result**

I love You

I Love

I Love book

## 4.8 Manipulate String Arrays

The previous sketch manually altered the string by reading individual characters in it. You may develop your functions or utilize some of the text functions from the C language library to make manipulating string arrays simpler.

## String()

The String class, which has been included in the core since version 0019, lets you utilize and modify text strings in more advanced ways than character arrays. Strings may be concatenated, appended to, searched for and replaced with substrings, and more. It consumes greater memory than a plain character array, and it is much more useful.

Character arrays are referenced as strings with a little 's,' while String class instances are referred to as strings with a capital S. Constant strings enclosed in "double quotes" be handled as char arrays rather than String objects.

## charAt()

Get a specific character from the String.

## compareTo()

Compares two Strings to see whether one is preceding or following the other or equal. The ASCII codes of the characters are used to compare the strings character by character. It indicates that 'a' comes preceding 'B' but after 'A,' for example. Numbers appear first, followed by letters.

## concat()

The argument is appended to a String.

## c_str()

Converts a string's contents to a null-terminated C-style string. It's worth noting that this provides you direct access to the internal String buffer, so use it with caution. In particular, you must never change the string using the returned reference. Any reference previously given by c str() becomes incorrect and should no longer be utilized when the String object is modified or destroyed.

### endsWith()

This function determines if a String terminates with characters from another String.

### equals()

Compares two strings to see whether they are equivalent. The string "hello" is not equivalent to the string "HELLO" since the comparison is case-sensitive.

### equalsIgnoreCase()

Compares two strings to see whether they are equivalent. The comparison is case-insensitive; thus String("hello") is the same as String("hello") ("HELLO").

### getBytes()

The characters of the string are copied to the buffer provided.

### indexOf()

Within another String, identifies a character or string. It searches at the start of the string by default, but it may alternatively start at a specific index to find all occurrences of the letter or string.

### lastIndexOf()

Within another String, it locates a word or string. It searches from the beginning of the string by default, but it may optionally move backward from a provided index to find all the letter or string occurrences.

### length()

It returns the total number of characters in a string.

### remove()

Remove characters from the specified index to an end of a string or from specified index till index plus counts in situ.

## replace()

Replace all occurrences of a specified character with some other character using the string replace () method. Replace may also be used to replace substrings in a string with another substring.

## reserve ()

The String reserve () method enables you to set up a memory buffer for string manipulation.

## setCharAt()

Sets one of the string's characters. Has no impact on indices that are longer than the string's current length?

## startsWith()

Checks if a string begins with characters from another String.

## toCharArray()

The characters of the string are copied to the buffer provided.

## substring()

Get a String's substring. The beginning index is inclusive (the substring contains the matching character), while the additional finishing index is exclusive (the corresponding words are not included in the substring). The segment continues to the end of a String if the terminating index is omitted.

## toInt()

Converts an integer from a valid String. An integer number should be the first character in the input string. The function will stop converting the string if it includes non-integer integers.

## toFloat()

A valid String is converted to afloat. A digit should be the first character in the input string. The function will stop converting the string if it includes non-digit characters. The strings "685.45", "685", and "685fish" are, for example, translated to 685.45, 685.00, and 685.00. It's worth noting that "685.45" is roughly equivalent to 685.45. It's also worth noting that floats only have 6-7 numeric accuracy values, and longer sequences may be truncated.

## toLowerCase()

A lowercase form of a Strings is returned. toLowerCase(), as of version 1.0, alters the existing string rather than producing a new one.

## toUpperCase()

The upper-case version of the string may be obtained. Instead of creating a new string, toUpperCase() alters the existing one as of version 1.0.

## trim()

Have a version of a String that doesn't include any leading or following whitespace. Trim(), as of version 1.0, alters the existing string instead of producing a new one.

## 4.9 Array Bounds

When working with strings and arrays, it is very important to work within the bounds of strings or arrays. In the example sketch, an array was created, which was 40 characters long, to allocate the memory used to manipulate strings.

If the array were made too small and tried to copy a bigger string than the array, the string would be copied over the end of the array. The memory beyond the end of the array could contain other important data used in the sketch, which our string would then overwrite. If the memory beyond the end of the string is overrun, it could crash the sketch or cause unexpected behavior.

## 4.10 String Object

The String Object is the second form of text used in Arduino programming.

### What is an Object?

A construct that comprises all functions and data is known as an object. A String object may be created and assigned a string or value in the same way as a variable. The String object has functions (also known as "methods" of object-oriented programming (OOP)) that act on the String object's string data.

The accompanying diagram and explanation will demonstrate what an object is or how to utilize the String object.

```
void setup () {
  String my_string= "Object string.";
  Serial.begin(9600);   // (1) print the string
  Serial.println(my_string);   // (2) change the string to upper-case
my_string.toUpperCase();
  Serial.println(my_string);   // (3) string overwrite
my_string = "New object.";
  Serial.println(my_string);
  my_string.replace("Object", "string");
  Serial.println(my_string);
```

```
    Serial.print("Object length is: ");

    Serial.println(my_str.length());

}

void loop() {

}
```

Result

Object string

OBJECT STRING

New Object.

New String.

Object length is 10

A string object is built and given a value (or string) at the top of the sketch. a line

```
my_string= "Object string.";
```

It constructs a String object called my_str and assigns the value "Object string." to it.

It is analogous to defining a variable & assigning it a value, such as an integer.

int My_Num = 108;

The following is how the sketch works.

The string is printed. Like a character array string, the string may be displayed to the Serial Monitor window.

Change the string's case to uppercase. Some various methods or functions may be used on the string object my str that was generated. These methods are called by first typing the object's name, then the dot operator (.), and finally the function's name.

`My_stringtoUpperCase();`

The toUpperCase() method turns the string (or text) in the str object of type String to upper-case characters. The Arduino Strings reference contains a list of a function in the String class. A string is technically referred to as a class, and it is utilized to construct String instances.

**Overwrite a String**

An assignment operator is being used to replace the existing string.

My_string = "New string." with a new string.

**Substituting a Word in a String**

The replace() method replaces the first string with the second string that is provided to it. Replace () is another String class method that may be used mostly on String object My_string.

**Length of the String**

Using length to determine the length of the text is simple (). The length() value is delivered straight to Serial. println() in the sample sketch without requiring an intermediary variable.

**Use a String Object**

A string text array is substantially more difficult to utilize than a String object. The object comes with built-in functions which can manipulate strings in a variety of ways.

The String object's biggest downside is that it consumes an amount of storage and may soon exhaust the Arduino's memory, causing the Arduino to stall, crash, or act strangely. There must be no issues if an Arduino program is modest and restricts the usage of objects.

Text array strings are much more complex to work with, and you may have to build your routines to manipulate them. The benefit is that you can regulate the size of the text arrays you create, allowing you to keep them short and conserve memory.

With string arrays, you must ensure that you do not write past the limits of the array. It is not an issue for the String object, which will take good care of the string boundaries for you whether there is enough space for it to work with. When the String object runs out of memory, it may try to write into memory that doesn't exist, but it will never write beyond the end of the string it's working with.

You learned about strings in this chapter, including how they operate in memory and how to manipulate them.

## 4.11 Arrays

An array is a data structure of memory regions of the same kind that are arranged logically. The name of an array and the position integer of the individual elements in the array is used to refer to a specific place or element in the array.

An integer array named C with 11 members is shown in the diagram below. You may refer to any of these elements by putting the array name in square brackets, followed by the element's position number ([]). A subscript or index is the official name for the position number (this number specifies the number of elements from the beginning of the array). The initial element is commonly referred to as the zeros element since it bears the subscript 0 (zero).

C[0] (pronounced "C subzero"), C[1], C[2], and so forth are the components of array C. In array C, the maximum subscript is 10, which is less than the array's total number of items (11). The same rules apply to array names as they do to variable names.

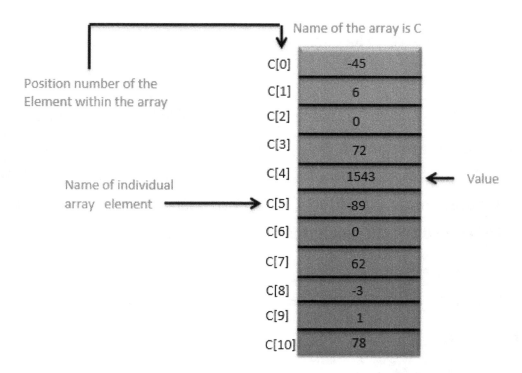

An integer or an integer expression must be used as a subscript (using any integral type). If a system needs an integer as a subscript, the subscript is determined by evaluating the expression. For instance, if variable an equals five and variable b equals 6, two to array item C[11].

An lvalue is a subscripted array name that may be used on the left side of an assignment in the same way as non-array variable names.

Let's take a closer look at array C in the diagram. The complete array is referred to as C. C [0] to C[10] are the 11 components that make up this compound. C[0] has a value of -45, C[1] has a value of 6, C[2] has a value of 0, C[7] has a value of 62, and C[10] has a value of 78.

You would write Serial. Print (C[ 0 ] + C[ 1 ] + C[ 2 ] ); to display the total of the values contained during the first three items of array C.

You would write y = C[ 6 ] / 2 to divide C[6] by two and result in the variable y.

## 4.12 Declaring Arrays

Arrays take up memory. Use the type array_Name[]

The compiler sets aside the necessary amount of RAM. (It's worth noting that a declaration that saves memory is more appropriately referred to as a definition.) The array size parameter must be a non-zero integer constant. Use the declaration int C [ 10]; / C is an array of 10 integers to inform the compiler to reserve ten members for integer array C.

Items of any non-reference type of data may be defined in arrays. An array of type strings, for example, may be used to hold character strings.

## 4.13 Interrupts

Interrupts cause Arduino's present operation to pause so that other tasks may be completed. Let's pretend you're at home, conversing with someone. The phone suddenly rings. You put down the phone and take it up to talk with the caller. When you've ended your phone discussion, you return to conversing with the person with whom you were conversing before the phone rang.

Similarly, imagine the primary routine as speaking with someone, with the phone ringing interrupting your conversation. The process of chatting on the phone is known as the interrupt service routine. When the phone call is over, you return to your usual talking routine. This example shows how a interrupt forces a processor to respond.

In a circuit, the primary program is running and performs some functions. However, when an interrupt occurs, the main program comes to a stop while another procedure is executed. When these routines are completed, the processor returns to the main Procedure.

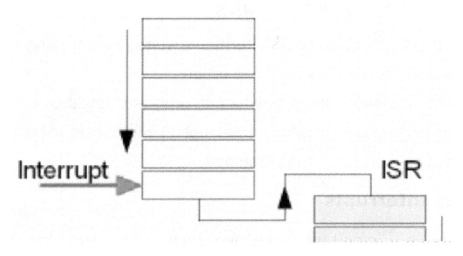

## Important features

Here are some key characteristics of interrupts:

- Interruptions may occur from a variety of causes. A hardware interrupt is used in this situation, generated by a state change on one of the digital pins.
- The hardware interrupts "interrupt0" and "interrupt1" are hard-wired to digital I/O pins 3 and 2, respectively, in most Arduino designs.
- The Arduino Mega includes six hardware interrupts, including extra interrupts on pins 21, 20, 19, and 18 ("interrupt2" through "interrupt5").
- A specific function named "Interrupt Service Routine" may be used to create a routine (usually known as ISR).
- You have the option of defining the routine and specifying criteria for the rising, falling, or both edges. The Interrupt would've been served in these circumstances.

- It's feasible to get that function run automatically whenever an event on to an input pin occurs.

## 4.14 Types of Interrupts

Interrupts are divided into two categories.

- External events, including an alternating voltage pin turning high or low, cause hardware interrupts to occur.
- Software Interrupts happen when a program sends a command to another program. The attach Interrupt () method is the sole sort of Interrupt supported by the "Arduino language."

## 4.15 Using Interrupts

Interrupts are very important in Arduino applications since they aid in the resolution of timing issues. Reading a rotating encoder or watching a user input is a nice example of utilizing an interrupt. An ISR should, in general, be as brief and quick as feasible. Only one ISR may run at a time if your drawing has several ISRs. Other interruptions will be performed because their priority determines the order after the current one has been completed.

It transmits the data between ISR and the main program, and global variables are often employed. Declare variables shared with an ISR and the primary program as volatile to ensure they are updated appropriately.

The valid values for the three following constants are predefined:

- LOW When the Pin is low, the Interrupt is triggered.
- CHANGE will cause the Interrupt to be triggered the value of the pin changes anytime.
- FALLING: the Pin is moved from a high to a low position.

## 4.16 Due & Zero

An Arduino Due is an ARM Cortex-M3 board is based upon an Atmel SAM3X8E processor. It will be the first Arduino to use a microprocessor with a 32-bit ARM core.

**Important features**

- There are 54 digital input/output pins on it (of which 12 can be used as PWM outputs)
- 4 UARTs
- 12 analog inputs (hardware serial ports)
- 84 MHz clock and USB OTG connectivity
- Reset and erase buttons
- 2 DAC (digital into analog), 2 TWI, a voltage connector, an SPI header, and a JTAG header

**Communication**

UARTs in hardware, 2 I2C, 1 CAN Interfaces (Automotive communication protocol), 1 SPI, 1 JTAG (10 pins) Interface, 1 USB Host (similar to Leonardo), and 1 Programming Port

The Arduino Due board, unlike other Arduino boards, operates at 3.3V. The I/O pins can withstand a maximum voltage of 3.3V. Any I/O pin that receives a voltage greater than 3.3V may be damaged.

The board comes with everything you'll need to get started with the microcontroller. To get started, just plug it into a computer using a micro-USB connection or power it using an AC-to-DC converter or battery. All Arduino shielding that functions at 3.3V is compatible with the Due.

## 4.17 Arduino Zero

The Zero is a 32-bit expansion of the UNO's platform that is both simple and powerful. The Zero board adds to the family by increasing performance, allowing for a wider range of device projects, and serving as a wonderful instructional tool to learn about 32-bit programming.

**Important features**

- The board is controlled by Atmel's SAMD21 MCU, which has a 32-bits ARM Cortex M0+ core and may be used for wearable technology, smart IoT devices, high-tech automation, and wacky robots. Atmel's Embedded Debugger (EDBG) is one of its most essential features since it offers a comprehensive debug interface without any need for extra hardware, greatly simplifying software debugging. • EDBG also offers a virtual COM port that may be used for devices and bootloader programming.

- The Zero operates at 3.3V, unlike other Arduino and Genuine boards. The I/O pins can withstand a maximum voltage of 3.3V. Any I/O pin that receives a voltage greater than 3.3V may be damaged.

- The board comes with everything you'll need to get started with the microcontroller. To get started, just plug it into a computer using a micro-USB connection or use an AC-to-DC converter or a battery. All shields that function at 3.3V are compatible with the Zero.

## 4.18 Arduino – Communication

It facilitates data interchange, dozens of communication protocols are being established. Each protocol may be classified into one of two groups: parallel or serial.

**Parallel Communication**

For shorter distances of up to a few meters, the parallel circuit between the Arduino with peripheral through i/o ports is the best option. Parallel connection is not practicable in some instances, such as when the conversation between multiple devices must be established across larger distances. Parallel interfaces allow several bits to be sent at the same time. They frequently need data buses, which transfer data across sixteen, twelve, or more wires. The data is sent in massive, crashing waves of 1s and 0s.

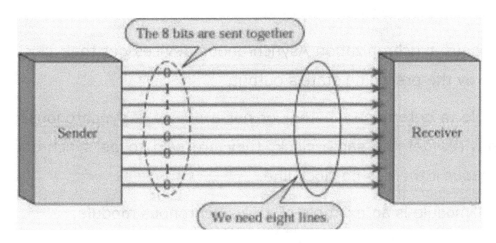

## Advantages/ disadvantages

Parallel communication provides a lot of benefits. It's quicker than serial, more intuitive, and simpler to implement. It does, however, need a large number of (I/O) connections and lines. If you've ever had to upgrade a project from a simple Arduino Board to a Mega, you know how valuable and limited the I/O lines on a CPU can be. As a result, You choose serial communication over parallel communication, sacrificing compelling for pin real estate.

## Serial Communication

Most Arduino boards now come with a variety of serial connection methods as standard equipment. One of the most crucial aspects of serial communication is the Procedure, which must be followed to the letter. It is just a set of rules for the devices to comprehend the data they communicate appropriately.

Fortunately, Arduino takes care of this automatically, reducing the programmer's/effort users to basic write (data to be transferred) and read operations (received data).

## Serial Communications Types

Serial communication is further subdivided into the following categories:

synchronized devices that are synchronized utilize the same schedule, and their time is in sync with one another.

Asynchronous synchronization Asynchronous devices get their clock and are activated by the preceding state's output.

It is simple to determine whether or not a device is synchronous. When all linked devices get the same clock, they are said to be synchronous. It is asynchronous if there is no clock line.

The UART module is an example of an asynchronous module.

There are many built-in rules in the asynchronous serial protocol. These principles are nothing more than methods that aid in the reliable and error-free transmission of data. These mechanics are what You get when You don't use an external clock signal.

## Bits of Synchronization

Each data packet contains two or three synchronization bits, which are 2 or 3 special. The start and stop bits are what they're called (s). These bits, as their names suggest, indicate the start and end of a packet.

Only one start bit is always present, but the number of stop bits may be set to 1-2 (though it is normally left at one).

An idle data line traveling from 1 to 0 always indicates the start bit, whereas the stop bit(s) will keep the line at one and return smoothly to the idle state.

synchronicity a few bits

## Bits of information

Each packet's data size may be adjusted anywhere between 5 and 9 bits. The usual data size is an 8-bit byte, although another size has its applications as well. When just sending 7-bit ASCII letters, a 7-bits data packet may be more effective than an 8-bit data packet.

## Bits of Parity

The user may choose if a parity bit should be present and if the parity should be even or odd. If the amount of 1s in the bytes is even, the parity is 0. Odd parity is the polar opposite of even parity.

## Baud Rate (Baud Rate)

The number of bits transmitted per second [bps] is referred to as baud rate. It's important to note that it's talking about bits, not bytes. Each byte must normally be sent with numerous control bits, as dictated by the protocol. It indicates that a single byte in a serial data stream might be 11 bits long. For example, if such baud rate is 300 bps, the maximum and minimum bytes sent per second are 37 and 27, respectively.

# Conclusion

My friends, this small book has already come to an end. Although I hope that you will be able to use Arduino programming "off the shelf" in your industry, you will be satisfied if it only stimulates your interest. The techniques outlined in this book are among the most effective ways for Arduino programmers of all levels to improve their performance and expertise. Consider how you and your coworkers will and can utilize them – and other tools that will become available – to boost efficiency. This book is written for Arduino novices and pros who want to learn how to program the board from the ground up. You have attempted to cover the following topic in this book, which is equally important for beginners and professionals.

- Obtain the appropriate Arduino hardware and peripherals for your requirements.

- Download and install the Arduino IDE, then connect it to your Arduino.

- Create, develop, upload, and execute your first Arduino program quickly and easily.

- Understand C grammar, decision-making, strings, data functions and structures

- To operate with memory and prevent typical blunders, use pointers.

- Create development and testing environments, use development and testing shields, and functionality electronics to your Arduino

- Use existing hardware library functions or create your own

- Send output and publish input from analog devices or digital interfaces

- Install an Ethernet shield, install an Ethernet cable, and write a networking program

www.ingramcontent.com/pod-product-compliance
Lightning Source LLC
Chambersburg PA
CBHW060204060326
40690CB00018B/4243